After Action Review

Continuous Improvement *Made Easy*

Artie Mahal

Technics Publications

Published by:

2 Lindsley Road
Basking Ridge, NJ 07920 USA
https://www.TechnicsPub.com

Edited by Lauren McCafferty
Cover design by Lorena Molinari
Artie Mahal's photograph taken by Bryan S. Passione

First Printing 2018
Copyright © 2018 by Artie Mahal

ISBN, print ed.	9781634623230
ISBN, Kindle ed.	9781634623247
ISBN, ePub ed.	9781634623254
ISBN, PDF ed.	9781634623261

Library of Congress Control Number: 2017964494

To the United States of America

In gratitude to my adopted country, which gave me
opportunities to learn, develop, and excel, both personally and
professionally.

Contents

Foreword

What did we do well? And how can we replicate that so we can repeat it time and time again?

What did not go well? And how can we prevent that from ever happening again?

Fairly simple questions. But if we focus on the answers, they provide us with a pathway to future success. After nearly every activity, asking these questions during a time of reflection is necessary and important. We want to continuously repeat the behaviors and actions that result in positive results or rewards. We want to learn from mistakes, and prevent these from happening again.

Whether this time of reflection is done at the completion of a multi-million-dollar project impacting hundreds of stakeholders, or after a personal Do It Yourself (DIY) project you took on at home, this reflection helps us enforce the good behaviors and prevent the bad ones. It forces us to confront our mistakes with the goal of learning from them, and hopefully never repeating them again. This process reinforces and celebrates the good behaviors, thus increasing the chance of repeating those, while pointing out the bad behaviors to prevent these from recurring. It sounds easy enough…but to do it well requires the right mix of science and art.

Getting that mix of science and art just right is the key. My good friend and colleague Artie Mahal has done us all a favor by writing this book about how to best perform After Action Reviews. In this book, he provides us with the secret of getting that mix just right. As someone who has dedicated his life's work to helping organizations work better, smarter, and more efficiently, Artie has opened up his "tool box" for us. In this book, he provides us with a methodology to help us learn from the lessons of having completed a task or major project. What he points out to us is that the beauty of the process is that it is fairly simple and straightforward, but it requires the discipline to do it right. Artie has provided us with the tools to help us get it right the first, and every, time.

I have known Artie for over 25 years. We were colleagues at Mars, Incorporated for several years, and since then I have tapped into his knowledge and expertise for Process Management, Facilitation skills, and After Action Reviews several times. He has a passion for these topics, and is a natural at helping organizations increase their effectiveness. I'm grateful that he has taken the time to share some of his established and proven processes with all of us. You will be too. And your entire organization will benefit greatly from utilizing the practices spelled out in this wonderful book.

Paul Marabella
Vice President and Chief Information Officer
K. Hovnanian Companies, LLC.

Acknowledgements

In your career, you meet people who educate and inspire you in a way that instills not only new ways of thinking but also the confidence to take on the road to success. In addition to my gratitude to Mars, Incorporated for giving me numerous opportunities to learn and grow, I am deeply indebted to my colleagues and students who taught me through challenge and discourse on topics of professional interest.

My special thanks to Mike Foresman, a colleague and friend, with whom, as a "Dream Team" we jointly facilitated many workshops and conducted numerous After Action Reviews for clients in North America and elsewhere.

My editor, Lauren McCafferty, has been instrumental in not only correcting my grammar and sentence structures, but also suggesting ideas to make the flow of this professional "story" better. I am grateful to her for her contribution.

My publisher and friend, Steve Hoberman, and his staff have been once again a pleasure to work with and deserve my heartfelt thanks.

Last but not least, I thank my wife Millie for supporting my effort in publishing this book — as she has done for my previous writing adventures.

Introduction

From the beginning of time, humans have survived and thrived by learning from their experiences — both good and bad — and then tweaked their actions for better results next time. This continual quest for improvement stems from the difference between "what was" and "what could be possible."

Even if we're not consciously aware of it, we're constantly seeking improvement in this very same way. If we turn to this analysis in a more intentional and methodical way, with an eye towards continuous improvement, then next time around the outcomes can be more rewarding and desirable.

Through this art and science of applying learned knowledge, humans have advanced through innovation and invention. This same improvement mentality has led us from good to better in our products, our goods, our services, our processes, and just about everything we do, use, or create. This process is called continuous improvement (CI). Every aspect of our lives — including commerce, science, medicine, military, arts, and uncountable other fields — has improved through the CI process. An essential CI technique is the After Action Review (AAR).

The AAR is a structured approach for reflecting on the work of a group or team. By undertaking AAR, we methodically capture knowledge about an activity: of what was expected, what really happened, and how it can be improved for better results next time. This could also mean identifying strengths, weaknesses, and gaps that must be addressed.

The air force and the military pioneered this method of AAR in combat missions. When an airplane would come back from a sortie, the commanders would immediately conduct an AAR. This allowed them to learn about the conditions in the enemy area, so that the next sorties could adjust their attack approach—for better outcomes.

There are two aspects of the AAR approach: *Informal* and *Formal*. The informal approach is easy to use and can be carried out ad hoc, at virtually any time or place, without much preparation. The formal approach requires methodical preparation in advance and consumes more time.

In both of these approaches, the AAR is conducted with the stakeholders who were a part of the given activity, and would have a vested interest in continuous improvement for even better results next time. The person leading the AAR session is referred to as the facilitator or session leader. They can be one of the stakeholders, but ideally should be an external person who can remain neutral and has practiced facilitation of the AAR process.

Upon completion of any activity, the organizational stakeholders must ask these questions: What do we have to lose by **not** learning from the recent experience and the result? Conversely, what do we have to gain by improving outcomes next time around? Simply put, the answer to these questions is the *Value Proposition* of the After Action Review.

This book is meant for everyone who has interest in learning to use the AAR process with an eye towards improving an activity, event, project, product, service, or situation for just about anything, anywhere. Once you learn the use of both *Informal* and *Formal* AAR, this process will become second nature as a tool for capturing knowledge and continuously improving all aspects of human endeavors.

Best wishes,

Artie Mahal

CHAPTER 1
Techniques

In order to plan and conduct an After Action Review, it is essential to know some basic facilitation techniques. These foundational techniques are outlined in this chapter at the introductory level only. Each of these techniques could be a chapter or even a book by itself. There are numerous books and resources already available for the practitioner of After Action Review to further develop their skills.

For the *Informal* AAR, one does not have to have the mastery of these skills, but for the *Formal* AAR, the facilitator must be qualified and experienced to carry on the facilitation process more professionally. While organization and project management skills are basic to managing any activity, it is presumed that anyone planning to learn and conduct AAR must have some experience in managing work.

FACILITATION

While the term can have many meanings, *facilitation* is the art and craft of enabling individuals and groups to discuss issues and opportunities around a shared objective and develop agreed strategies for a common direction.

In addition to meetings, facilitation also includes enabling people to learn through transfer of knowledge and training in specific skills by a subject matter expert. The person skilled in facilitation is call a ***Facilitator***. The method for creating agendas, conducting research, and facilitating sessions to deliver planned outputs and outcomes is referred to as the ***Facilitation Process***.

The facilitation process uses a variety of frameworks, methods, techniques, and tools. Skilled facilitators use a combination of these tools along with several other methods that include managing group dynamics, managing the time and process, and leading the sessions to successful conclusions.

Some of these tools are general in nature and applicable to many scenarios, such as *Icebreakers* for meetings. There are also techniques and tools specific to professional practices, such as the Stakeholder Analysis used for improving products and services in an organization. Facilitators possess a set of specific training tools for their subject matter to ensure the knowledge transfer is effective.

In some large organizations, facilitators are provided by human resource functions, learning and development departments, and other functional areas around specialized Centers of Excellence. In some organizations, however, all line and senior managers are expected to have facilitation skills.

Facilitating is a role and typically not a job title. Organizations that define and nurture facilitation as one of the core competencies for their managers have both improved and sustainable outcomes in their initiatives and solutions, and developed employees' leadership attributes.

To run and win a race, the horse needs a skilled jockey. Facilitators are the organizational *"jockeys"* that lead the *"race horses"*—the work groups—to optimize their success.

FOUNDATIONAL SKILLS

The following seven foundational skills are essential for anyone in the role of a facilitator. To develop these skills, facilitators need to be aware of their personal strengths and weaknesses and then diligently work to acquire and practice those competencies. *Facilitators must be at their best while facilitating sessions.* This is the measure of their competency:

- ✓ Active listening
- ✓ Questioning
- ✓ Information gathering and analysis
- ✓ Public speaking
- ✓ Presenting
- ✓ Intervening
- ✓ Managing group dynamics

ACTIVE LISTENING

Epictetus, the Greek sage and philosopher (AD55-135) stated:

> *Nature gave us one tongue and two ears so that we could hear twice as much as we speak.*

The idea that we should be good listeners has a profound meaning for anyone in the role of a facilitator. After all, facilitation is really all about helping people listen to one another, and the facilitator is included. The following Listening Ladder technique can be easily mastered with practice.

The Listening Ladder

Look	Look at the person speaking to you. Make eye contact to express that you are interested in what the other person has to say.
Ask	Ask questions. Ask follow-up open-ended questions to comprehend the meaning of what is being said by the speaker.
Don't	Don't interrupt or be interrupted. Ensure that the interruption is only for clarification of what has been said.
Don't	Don't change the subject. You will get an indication to change the topic when the speaker is finished with one thought. Look for cues to transition to another topic.
Empathize	Empathize with the speaker. Demonstrate this by a gesture such as "nodding your head" so that the speaker sees that you are interested in what is being said.
Respond	Respond verbally and nonverbally. Through body language such as nodding your head, eye/eyebrow movements, acknowledge that you are just as engaged in the conversation as the speaker is. You can do this without interrupting the speaker by saying, "...I see..." or "...I understand..."

Here is an exercise to demonstrate the value of good listening in team building or work sessions.

Process

1. *Team Formation*: Ask participants to pair up.

2. *Instruction*: Have Person One tell a story about any topic to Person Two. Person One is the speaker and Person Two is the listener. Instruct Person Two to not pay any attention to what Person One says. Instruct Person One to begin telling the story for one minute only.

3. *Debrief*: After Step #2 is complete, ask Person One how they felt. The usual response is, "Person Two was disengaged and not interested in what I had to say. It was uncomfortable to go on telling my story."

4. *The Listening Ladder*: Now explain the concept of the Listening Ladder as an awareness and skill-building tool. Have the pairs repeat the exercise in Step #2, but this time, ask Person Two to apply Listening Ladder principles in the conversation with Person One.

5. *Debrief*: Ask Person One and Person Two how they both felt in this exchange. The typical response is that Person One is satisfied that their story was conveyed well. Usually Person Two expresses that they were fully engaged and interested in what Person One had to say.

QUESTIONING

Asking the right questions about a topic of interest by anyone is very important. For a facilitator, the art of developing questions is a critical skill. At the time of engagement of an assignment, asking the right questions establishes a productive relationship with the client to gain a clear understanding of expectations.

To solicit the right information from the stakeholder interviews, the facilitator must develop specific and comprehensive questions. During sessions, facilitators continually ask questions of the participants to engage them in promoting appropriate discussions and assisting in the decision-making process. Moreover, occasionally, groups need to formulate questions to address the support of new products and services being planned. The following tools are practical for developing questions by an individual or in a group setting.

APPRECIATIVE INQUIRY

Appreciative Inquiry (AI) is an organization development tool that promotes asking questions in a positive way, such as, "What worked well in the past?" and "What might be possible in the future?" rather than focusing on "What is wrong?" It is a philosophical approach of focusing on what is good (and can be better) instead of dwelling on problems alone.

Developed and extended since the mid-eighties primarily by students and faculty of the Department of

Organizational Behavior at Case Western Reserve University, AI revolutionized the field of organization development and was a precursor to the rise of positive organization studies and the strengths-based movement in American management. In the original 1987 article on AI by David Cooperrider and Suresh Srivastva, they argued that the overuse of problem solving reduced the ability of managers and researchers to come up with new theories and models of organizing. More details on this topic are widely available elsewhere.

Here I want to show you a practical application of how you may create questions using the AI technique.

Sue Annis Hammond, in *The Thin Book of Appreciative Inquiry*, has identified eight assumptions that simplify the understanding of AI's application:

1. In every society, organization, or group, something works.

2. What we focus on becomes our reality.

3. Reality is created in the moment, and there are multiple realties.

4. The act of asking questions of an organization or group influences the group in some way.

5. People have more confidence and comfort to journey to the future (the unknown) when they carry forward parts of the past (the known).

6. If we carry parts of the past forward, they should represent the very best aspects of the past.

7. It is important to value differences.

8. The language we use creates our reality.

Here are some sample questions using Appreciative Inquiry:

- Describe a time when you felt that your colleagues collaborated among each other really well as a team.

- Describe a time when you were proud to be a member of that team. Why were you proud?

- What do you value most about being a member of that team? Why?

Questions framed in this way provide profound insights of what has been good and can be even better.

KIPLING'S "FRAMEWORK"

I have found that for formulating questions for *any* purpose, Rudyard Kipling's poem *The Elephant's Child* provides a practical framework that works every time. Born in Bombay, India (now Mumbai), Joseph Rudyard Kipling is considered one of the greatest English writers and was the recipient of the Nobel Prize for literature in 1907. Here's an excerpt from The Elephant's Child:

I keep six honest serving-men

(They taught me all I knew);

Their names are What and Why and When

And How and Where and Who.

I send them over land and sea,

I send them east and west;

But after they have worked for me,

I give them all a rest...

The six words **What, Why, When, How, Where,** and **Who** are the basis of thinking through formulation of questions. As a facilitator, whether you are preparing for an interview with clients or stakeholders, or engaging session participants in a meaningful dialogue, Kipling's "six serving-men" are your friends indeed.

I have also used this framework of six words when I am asked to write a strategy or a position paper. The concept is simple yet powerful when you are starting to write on a blank piece of paper.

INFORMATION GATHERING AND ANALYSIS

Workshops typically consist of these stages: *information gathering, analyses and synthesis,* and *action plans.* These may vary according to the subject matter and professional practice situations being dealt with. Each of these is generic in nature and used in just about every methodology, technique, or tool one may encounter. Brainstorming types and the KJ Method are described in this section.

- *Brainstorming* is the first stage, with participants generating their ideas on the topic of focus on sticky notes—one idea per sticky note. It is a technique that helps groups to generate large amounts of information about any topic of interest, for the purpose of further analysis. It is typically followed by the KJ Method of clustering the information. This method is named after Jiro Kawakita who had devised this approach in 1960's.

- *Affinity Diagram (KJ Method)* is the next stage and is used to observe affinity among like ideas, and cluster them into themes relevant to the topic under study. This is a collaborative team effort to agree on the labels of the themes to make them meaningful to the audience. This technique helps organize large amounts of data/information into manageable, understandable themes and is used in conjunction with brainstorming. It is typically followed by further analysis and actions.

- *Analysis and Actions* is the third stage, where the team reaches agreement on the priority of these themes. This is important to decide how to allocate resources and implement agreed solutions. One method is *"Dotocracy,"* a democratic method where majority rules. A set of sticky dots (or simply "dots") of any color are distributed to the participants to vote on their personal preference. They can distribute the given set of dots across many clusters or they may place all of their dots on one cluster. This method is very common and is widely used in organizations, and depends on the professional practice and unique purpose of the analysis. Actions, initiatives, or projects may be created to achieve desired results.

Since brainstorming in its many forms is the most common tool used in meetings and work sessions for gathering information, idea generation, and problem solving, it is useful to understand its origin, theory, and the types of brainstorming that can be used in a variety of situations.

Advertising executive Alex F. Osborn began developing methods for creative problem solving in 1939. He was frustrated by employees' inability to develop creative ideas individually for ad campaigns. In response, he began hosting group-thinking sessions and discovered a significant improvement in the quality and quantity of ideas produced by employees. Osborn outlined the method in his 1953 book, *Applied Imagination.*

Brainstorming is a creativity technique that is used to find solutions to specific problems by gathering a list of ideas that are spontaneously contributed by its member(s). Osborn claimed that when it comes to generating ideas, having a group brainstorm was more effective than individuals working alone (although research that is more recent has brought this conclusion into debate). Today, the term is used as a catch all for all group ideation sessions.

Principles: Osborn claimed that two principles contribute to "ideative efficacy."

　1) Defer judgment

　2) Reach for quantity

Rules: Following these two principles were his four general rules of brainstorming, established with the intention to:

- Reduce social inhibitions among group members

- Stimulate idea generation

- Increase overall creativity of the group

Osborn's Four General Rules of Brainstorming

1. *Focus on quantity:* This rule is a means of enhancing divergent production, aiming to facilitate problem solving through the maxim "quantity breeds quality." The assumption is that the greater the number of ideas generated, the greater the chance of producing a radical and effective solution.

2. *Withhold criticism*: In brainstorming, criticism of ideas generated should be put on hold. Instead, participants should focus on extending or adding to ideas, reserving criticism for a later "critical stage" of the process. By suspending judgment, participants will feel free to generate unusual ideas.

3. *Welcome unusual ideas*: To get a good and long list of ideas, unusual ideas are welcomed. They come from looking at problems from new perspectives and suspending assumptions. These new ways of thinking may provide better solutions.

4. *Combine and improve ideas:* Good ideas may be combined to form a single "better" good idea, as suggested by the phrase "1+1=3." It is believed to stimulate the building of ideas by a process of association.

Osborn notes that brainstorming should address a specific question. He held that sessions addressing multiple questions were inefficient. Further, the problem must require the generation of ideas rather than judgment. For example, generating possible names for a product is a great activity for brainstorming. On the other hand, judgments such as whether or not to marry are not the best candidates for brainstorming.

Osborn envisioned groups of around twelve participants, including both experts and novices. Participants are encouraged to provide wild and unexpected answers.

Ideas receive no criticism or discussion. The group simply provides ideas that might lead to a solution and applies no analytical judgment of feasibility. The judgments are reserved for a later date and action.

If the group is very large then sub-teams can be formed to brainstorm a topic. The raw data can then be synthesized for collective result. For what might be an ideal size for a group to conduct brainstorming, I like the rule of thumb used by Amazon CEO Jeff Bezos, outlined by Dana Wright in her book *To Meet or NOT to Meet*? It's called "The Two Pizza Rule": If you have more people at a meeting (or a work session) than can be fed with two pizzas, then you have too many people.

Over the years there has been some criticism of the brainstorming technique in that individuals, when working in groups, may withhold their individual ideas and therefore "free ride" with others without fully participating, and thus undermine brainstorming. To prevent this possibility, ask the participants to first reflect on their own thoughts individually and then contribute their ideas to the larger group collectively.

PUBLIC SPEAKING

This is an enormous topic with hundreds of ideas and equal number of books available. Here I am outlining some basic yet effective speaking considerations that have worked for me every time.

LEARN TO LISTEN

Most people have poor listening skills. When someone is talking to us, we start thinking about what we are going to say next. The *Listening Ladder* described earlier in this chapter should be consciously kept in mind when engaging with anyone in any situation.

UNDERSTAND YOUR AUDIENCE

Before any speaking engagement, work with your sponsor to understand who would be the participants and what is important to them. Are there any hot spots you should avoid? Any topics that might be particularly sensitive to this crowd? Also, determine what kind of outcomes the audience would consider successful. Calibrate your goals to their expectations.

STRUCTURE YOUR MESSAGE

Craft the essence of your message and review it with your sponsor, to make certain it meets expectations. Ensure that there is a powerful opening, a meaningful middle and a memorable closing at the end. Try to avoid complicated words and phrases; simple language is better. Use of multimedia is appropriate as long as technology does not get in the way. Practice reading aloud your message several times before the speaking engagement to get the rhythm of the delivery. Include visuals to make your points.

CONNECTION BEFORE CONTENT

When you arrive at the venue, introduce yourself and shake hands. Depending upon the topic of the talk, include some metaphors and stories that would provide the context to the audience and would grab their attention. In a multi-lingual audience, it is always better to learn a word or two to speak in the local language of the audience.

STYLE

The style of the speaker can have several dimensions:

- **Attire**. Dress professionally to suit the occasion; check your appearance in the restroom to ensure your clothes and hair are presentable.

- **Non-verbal cues**. Be careful to avoid making non-verbal cues that could be interpreted as impatient or negative (e.g. glancing at your watch, looking outside through the window, or folding your arms).

- **Non-words**. Never use space-filling expressions such as "you know," "aaah," or "umm." Observe some of the best speakers and note that they rarely or never use these "non-words."

- **Posture and energy**. Always maintain an erect posture; continuously demonstrate energy and enthusiasm in your delivery (as the audience draws energy from the speaker). Your movements while talking should have a purpose. Rather than moving around on the stage, stay erect and grounded in one place and pivot your body left and right to face the audience.

- **Voice.** Use the power of pause to create an impressive dramatic effect when making a point. Put a little color in your voice. Use the sound of your voice to create a dramatic effect; it should be expressive and may go up and down in pitch and cadence.

- **Eye contact.** Eye contact is critical whether the audience numbers ten or fifty; each attendee must feel that you are addressing them individually. You accomplish this by scanning your eyes across the audience like a lighthouse and looking into their eyes. For this reason, speakers who wear glasses should have non-glare lenses. If there is glare on the lenses, the audience will disengage.

Toastmaster International (www.toastmasters.org) is a perfect organization to learn and enhance your speaking skills in a non-threatening environment. Their mission is stated as: *"We empower individuals to become more effective communicators and leaders."* They have chapters around the world.

PRESENTING

The subject of presentations can be lengthy and make for a very large chapter. In this section, my objective is to provide some basic presentation concepts and techniques that a facilitator should be aware of and use effectively.

- **Material organization.** Based on the topic to be covered, organize your material using the Four W's: *What* is the topic of focus? *Why* am I giving this presentation? *Who* is the audience? *What* is in it for them? It may help to think about the outcome you expect from the presentation and then work through the four W's.

- **Delivery framework.** There is an old saying about presentations: *Tell them what you are going to tell them; tell them; and then tell them what you told them.* This is a basic three-part framework. First, know your subject well and succinctly describe your topic to the audience to get them interested in what is about to be delivered to them. "Whet their appetite" using an attention grabber. Then deliver the topic in an engaging way so that it is not a lecture but instead a productive dialogue. Upon completion of the topic, summarize what you have presented highlighting the key takeaways. Create a memorable close.

- **Timing.** Winston Churchill once said, "I must apologize for making a rather long speech this morning. I didn't have time to prepare a short one!" Presentations can drag on if not properly planned and rehearsed for time. The rule of thumb is to prepare your presentation then cut it by fifty percent. It is probable that unforeseen factors could cut into your allotted time. The shorter the better.

- **Questions.** John Townsend of France's Master Trainer Institute offers a very practical approach to handling questions and interruptions. Many audience questions are not questions as much as requests for clarification or attempts to gain the spotlight. Facilitators must answer succinctly as follows:

Reflect	Back to the questioner what you thought was the question: "If I understand correctly, you're asking…" Depending on how the questioner reformulates the question, answer it or Deflect it.
Deflect	*Group*: "How does the rest of the group feel?" or "Has anyone else had a similar problem?" *Reflect*: (to one participant—perhaps a subject matter expert) "John you're an expert on this…what do you think?" *Reverse*: (back to the questioner) "You've probably done something like this before. What's your view?"

- **Flip charting**. Today, it is less common than it once was to have flip charts available in conference rooms. The prevailing notion is that facilitators have laptops to make their presentations using an overhead projector. While this sort of advancement in technology and automation certainly enhances productivity, it comes at some cost. It may be hard to quantify, but there's a certain satisfaction to grabbing a marker and scribbling down an idea on a giant flipchart; some sensation there is missing from a computer-based presentation. There is a place for being "high tech" and there is a place for being "high touch." Both are needed. A smart presenter, particularly in the role of facilitation, has flip charts available in order to create a visual impact when needed.

Prepare key charts in advance, and give a title to each chart. Write big and bold and use bullets for emphasis on key items. Use "highway writing," with large, clear font and a combination of capital and lower-case letters. Some studies suggest that multiple colors engage the right side of the brain, which promotes creative thinking. Speak loudly while writing as you will be facing away from the audience. Another strategy is to ask a volunteer write on the flip chart.

When I have to write rather fast, I tend to make spelling errors, which the audience likes to point out. I draw a round circle with a dot in the middle on one of the flip charts and state, "I have a high-tech spell checker. At the end of the session when I press the button, all my misspellings are corrected." Alternatively, I tell them with humor that Mark Twain felt sorry for people who could spell only one way! Participants laugh at these and no one complains about misspellings thereafter.

- **Engagers and energizers**. To engage the audience in the most effective manner use relevant metaphors, stories, and involve the audience with engaging exercises.

- **Checklist**. The solution to Murphy's Law of, "If something can go wrong—it will," is a checklist of supplies, preparing, and practicing the delivery of material in advance, and ensuring that the equipment works and the room is set up properly.

Helpful Hints

- Learn about your audience: who they are and what matters most to them.

- Avoid "death by PowerPoint." Minimize slides and maximize engagement through dialogue, stories, and interactive transfer of messages.

- Use voice with "color" showing emotion. Speak loudly to ensure everyone can hear you.

- Have high visibility marker colors on hand. "Bruise" colors (black, blue, purple, maroon, and brown) offer the best visibility. Avoid red markers to the extent possible (colorblind people cannot differentiate red from certain other colors).

- Check the facility, equipment, supplies, and arrangements beforehand.

- Before delivery: Practice, Practice, and Practice!

INTERVENING

In facilitation, there are many interventions that must be handled situation by situation. In the case of AAR, the most important technique is addressed here: **Root Cause Analysis.** When it is determined that something did not work well, then how should the participants go about finding the root cause?

Ishikawa diagrams (also called fishbone diagrams or cause-and-effect diagrams) were first used in the twenties (and later popularized by Kaoru Ishikawa in the sixties) and show the causes of a specific event. The Ishikawa diagram is used for discovering root causes of problems in a variety of situations. The topic may include products, services, or any other area in an organization that demands improvement. The causes are grouped into some logical themes for further analysis and actions.

The diagram template has the main topic identified on one end as the "head of a fish" and like the skeleton of a fish, there are side "bones" or areas to identify issues and cluster them into themes. The participants make the template, identifying one topic or problem area of focus. Then they brainstorm causes of the problem around each "bone" and cluster the causes into logical themes relevant to the topic. The themes can also be identified first if the topic of focus is very familiar to the participants. In the example below, the topic selected is "The recruiter is not providing quality talent." After the brainstorming is done, the team decides to identify some Quick Win actions to fix the problem in an agreed timeframe.

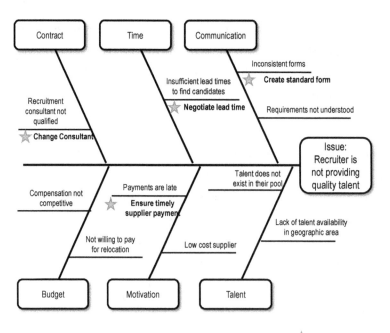

 Quick Wins

MANAGING GROUP DYNAMICS

A facilitator must develop good listening skills and learn to read the body language of the participants. Just as the lighthouse scans the horizon, so should be the facilitator continuously be aware of the level of engagement of the participants, be able to infer the meaning of the various behaviors, and intervene if needed. For example, if in a training workshop a participant seems to be uncomfortable with the topic of study, it is best to ask the group if they are comfortable with what was just covered. This gives participants opportunities to speak up and express what they are feeling. The same is true for any type of workshop. Some principles should be observed:

a) Never embarrass someone or put anyone on the spot by giving undue attention, regardless of their behavior.

b) Always maintain a professional composure and be matter of fact in dealing with the situation.

c) Always deal with the issue at hand, as a good leader would act diplomatically and not alienate anyone. Prior to your intervention, first determine whether the problem is a bad situation or a difficult and challenging participant. Some behaviors may be due to a genuine organizational urgency or a personal matter of the participant, such as childcare, elder care, or health issues.

d) Be aware of cross-cultural considerations.

For managing group dynamics, the concept of "Make the rounds, before you make the rounds" is critical, meaning that you must understand the personalities of all the stakeholders while planning the session engagement and designing the agenda.

The following Group Dynamics Guide outlines common people issues and strategies to deal with them in a workshop setting. These are by no means all the possible behaviors that can arise. However, with practice, you will become good at mastering all situations. Remember the Facilitator's Mantra: "Keep calm and carry on." This mantra is your best friend at all times.

Group Dynamics Guide

Dominating Participants:

Some Attributes	Strategy
• Backseat Driver has a habit of telling others what to do. • Broken Record repeats the same things over. • Loudmouth tries to show her importance. • Know It All has been in the organization a long time and shows off his knowledge. • Interpreter interprets what others say.	• Agree to session norms in the beginning and remind to the group as needed. • Maintain structured discussion on the topic. • Remain focused on the objectives and timeframes. • Encourage equal participation. • Ask the participant to write her issue on a sticky note, place it on the parking-lot chart, and address it later. • A one-on-one discussion may be necessary—in private.

The Skeptic:

Some Attributes	Strategy
• Late Comer / Early Leaver: Someone who wants to show his importance and may be of higher rank; or there may be a valid reason. • Attacker challenges every point without valid basis. Note: This type of behavior is common when there is an organizational change underway and the employees may be concerned about their job security or business change.	• Make sure the schedule is communicated. • Establish ground rule penalties for interruptions. • Communicate value of all participants' opinions and contribution. • Sometimes a one-on-one discussion may reveal that there is some business constraint or a personal issue that the participant is trying to deal with. This needs empathy and a different strategy to address the situation.

Making it Personal:

Some Attributes	Strategy
• Head Shaker repeatedly disagrees in a negative way. • Doubting Thomas has a negative view about things being addressed "this will never work…" • Dropout chooses to drop out of participating in important topic.	• Encourage feedback on the approach. • Enlist suggestions for change in the approach underway. • Try to clarify the reason for the course of discussion. • Do your homework on the personalities of the participants (i.e. *"make the rounds"*). • Ask the participant to come up to the flip chart and write their issue themselves.

The Sidebar:

Some Attributes	Strategy
• Whisperer • Gossiper • Busy Bee	• Physically move toward gossiping individuals (while carrying on with the topic) and ask: "are you all comfortable with what we are covering?" However, do not sound accusatory. • Ask for their input regarding the topic at hand. • Move on—don't embarrass them and find another way to engage them in a discussion.

Disengaged:

Some Attributes	Strategy
• Not participating actively • Blank look (Seems to not understand what is going on) • Disinterested Note: This type of behavior may be because of professional or person issues the individual might be going through at that time or s/he has been told by the superiors to be in the session without understanding the purpose and value to the individual.	• Try to engage this participant proactively in some activity such as writing on the flip chart. • Take a checkpoint on the progress being made in the session and that if everyone is comfortable with the activities. • A one-on-one discussion may be necessary—in private.

CREATING AN HONORABLE CLOSE TO THE WORKSHOP

Occasionally a work session may not go as planned. Due to various reasons, the session agenda may have to be drastically changed and even canceled by the manager or the sponsor. In such cases, the facilitator must always re-contract the agenda activities with the workshop manager/sponsor to accommodate any changes they might wish. The changed agenda may call for ending the workshop. If this occurs, the facilitator must begin wrapping up the closing items of the agenda (such as Next Steps, Communication Plan, and follow-up documentation).

Then thank the participants, and allow the manager or sponsor to formally close the workshop. This is an honorable way of wrapping up a session where unexpected issues cause it not to proceed further. Remember, the facilitator is responsible for the process and context, not the content. In conclusion, of this chapter, let me share with you *The Facilitator's Mantra* inspired by my colleague Vince Arecchi.

Facilitator's Mantra

Don't look for trouble

Throughout the facilitation process, pay attention to detail while keeping the big picture in mind. Stay within the professionalism of the art and craft of facilitation, and maintain upright behavior.

Don't let them see you sweat

The facilitator "stands alone" while facilitating a session. When unexpected situations arise, manage those wisely using tactics, honest responses, and integrity of intent. Always demonstrate self-confidence.

Keep calm and carry on

In any adverse situation, maintain your composure and deliver the agreed outcomes with patience, courage, and professionalism.

CHAPTER 2
After Action Review

After Action Review (AAR) is a technique of analyzing the results of any *Activity* by having the participant group members reflect on and acknowledge as to what was planned, what actually happened, and what could be improved next time around. This is a tool for continuous improvement (CI). An AAR can be conducted during the activity and definitely at the conclusion.

An *Activity* may be defined as the state or quality of being active; a specific deed, action, function or sphere of action.[1] For almost any organization, activities include meetings, work sessions, training classes and workshops, business initiatives, projects and programs, and

---

[1] Dictionary.com.

development of products and services. In non-profit organizations, for example, these could be fundraising activities. Within government, it could include policy development and implementation. In the case of Armed Forces, it could be battle strategies, preparations, and tactical actions. In the context of personal lives, it can be buying a property or a car, going on a vacation, or taking a cruise. The list is unlimited. The bottom line is that in just about in any activity or situation, an AAR can be a powerful tool for improvement and progress forward. The improvement may lead to doing things better, smarter, faster, more efficiently, or more effectively.

An AAR is centered on these questions for the activity in focus:

- What was planned and expected?

- What actually happened?

- What went well and what did not?

- What can we do better next time?

AAR features:

- Simple and inclusive of all participants. Everyone has a say.

- Non-threatening language. There is no finger pointing and the focus is on the common good.

- Identification of what was done well so that it can be repeated again.

- Open and honest discussion of what could be done better. Recommendations are in the form of lessons learned.

- Informal AAR can be conducted any time anywhere by anyone.

WHEN SHOULD THE AAR TOOL BE USED?

It is best to conduct AAR immediately after an activity has taken place and before the participants or project team disbands. This is a great opportunity for Informal AAR, as it can be spontaneous with little planning, and may take less than 20 to 30 minutes. On the other hand, Formal AAR needs detailed planning and can take more time. Depending on the scope of the project, the Formal AAR can take one to three days.

An AAR is a structured approach to managing knowledge and continuous improvement of any activity, project, or work session. It is also used to build a culture of accountability. This approach permits the participants of an activity to discover for themselves what happened and why. It can also be used to solicit ideas on how a particular activity could have been performed better. It should be conducted in response to some significant activity, or when an event in an organization has concluded.

The idea is to capture the learning immediately after the activity while the ideas are fresh in the minds of the participants as to what went well and what could be improved in the future. AARs are not critiques because they do not determine success or failure. They are professional discussions of activities and events with the intent of capturing knowledge and sharing it for future improvement.

The AAR, as an informal technique, may have existed from time immemorial and been used by battlefield commanders to learn from the mistakes made during the action and to plan their tactics for the next action, based on the learning.

The United States Army formally developed this technique during the early eighties as a "lesson learned" system. Over time, these have morphed into an efficient and effective process for correcting mistakes in future endeavors from the lesson learned and for sustaining success. This technique is generally conducted in group sessions, but it can be used in interview settings as well.

There are two types of AARs: *Informal* and *Formal*. Informal reviews are typically done after any activity including meetings, work sessions, or training sessions. These can be facilitated by one of the team members, who must be neutral in conducting this short session. They are conducted on the spot, immediately after the close of the event.

Formal reviews are themselves planned Activities. Relevant and key stakeholders are invited to a facilitated session that may be designed and conducted by a neutral and independent facilitator. They are done for large initiatives such as the launch of a product or service, the building of a structure, the rolling out of new strategies, and for processes and technology. This type of session may be held over several days. The sessions are conducted under the sponsorship of the senior executive responsible for the overall program or activity of focus.

VALUE PROPOSITION OF AAR

Value includes learning and insights of the completed activity through a methodical approach, further possibilities and opportunities for improvement and change, sense of accomplishment by all stakeholders, and developmental opportunities for people and processes. If an AAR is not conducted, clearly it is a loss of all the above benefits and further loss of resources and opportunities by repeating the same mistakes.

AFTER ACTION REVIEW FRAMEWORK

As shown in the figure on the next page, AAR comprises three stages.

Stage 1 - Individual Reflections

The individuals directly involved in a given activity are asked to think of these four questions:

- What were you trying to do?

- What actually happened?

- What did you like?

- What would you do differently?

This helps the individuals to frame their thoughts without any external influence.

Stage 2 - Group Insights

This is where all the participants and stakeholders of an activity collectively discuss the lessons learned, and frame ideas for improvement and change going forward.

Stage 3 - Recommend Improvements

From the lessons learned and ideas for the future, the whole group or an assigned subset would make a formal report and recommendation for change. This can sometimes take more time, because in some cases a feasibility study may have to be done before recommendation.

This is generally where the AAR Process ends. As a rule, action items and specific changes to implement are not products of AAR. Some other projects may be kicked off to actually implement the ideas discussed in the AAR.

CRITERIA FOR INFORMAL VERSUS FORMAL AAR

Informal	✓ Ad hoc (without much pre-work) ✓ Can be conducted for any activity of generally shorter duration such as staff meetings, problem solving sessions, and community events ✓ Someone with basic experience in group presentation/facilitation can conduct an AAR session with basic knowledge of the process ✓ Takes less time, usually anywhere from 15 minutes to a couple of hours ✓ Immediate improvement of ideas and opportunities for change can be gained
Formal	✓ Needs thorough planning and preparation ✓ Can be conducted for activities with bigger scope and of longer durations such as construction of a factory or a new product release ✓ Experienced facilitator with knowledge of AAR tool and process is required ✓ Takes time depending upon the scope of the activity, taking from one to three days of facilitation with about one week of planning and preparation ✓ While some quick wins can be identified immediately, the bigger improvement opportunities may take longer time

CHAPTER 3
Informal After Action Review

The following template is worded in a manner that facts can be expressed honestly without offending anyone or pointing fingers at anyone. To apply this technique, the facilitator prompts the participants to address these key questions:

- What was planned?

- What actually occurred? (Remember to look at facts and not judgments.)

- What went well and why?

- What can be improved and how?

APPROACH

Identify and gain agreement on the topic for the After Action Review assessment. Describe what was planned, what actually occurred and then conduct a brainstorming exercise with the participants. Two approaches can be used for gathering information.

INDIVIDUAL REFLECTION

Provide orientation to the participants in doing their individual assessment of what worked well and what can be done differently in the future. Furthermore, explain to them that after their individual assessment, a group brainstorming would be conducted to generate collective insights on the topic of lessons learned with an eye towards making recommendations for actions. The following template can be provided as pre-work or used in the real-time work session:

Individual Reflection

Name:

Activity Date:

What were you trying to do? (the scope of the activity)
What actually happened? (facts, feelings, and perceptions)
What did you like? (success factors, and results)
What would you differently? (ideas for improvement and change)

GROUP INSIGHTS

Three formats are examples of what templates can be used by the facilitator. This depends on the facilitator's preference, time allocated, and willingness of the participants.

Approach A:

    a. Frame the definition of an After Action Review for the participants and conduct the assessment.

    b. On a flip chart, create a template with two columns: **I Liked** and **I Wish**. These terms used as titles encourage a positive dialogue and avoid any blame-game.

I Liked	I Wish

Example of a training workshop:
 	
  • *I liked the content of the topic*
  • *...*
	Example of a training workshop:
	
	  • *I wish there were more visuals in the material*
	  • *...*

Example of a group session:
 	
  • *I liked the agenda design*
  • *...*
	Example of a group session:
	
	  • *I wish the facilitator had allowed more time for exercises*
	  • *...*

c. Prioritize the items "I Liked" and "I Wish" with the help of the participants. Facilitate a discussion to identify the solutions for improvement. Document their answers and rationale. In some cases, the participants can be assigned follow-up tasks to deliver those improvement solutions—right in that session. In other cases, a project manager may determine who will work on determining the solutions later.

d. Identify next steps for how the learning will be documented and communicated to all relevant stakeholders and others who would benefit from these improvements.

e. Thank the participants and close the AAR session.

f. After the workshop, summarize the AAR result and communicate to relevant stakeholders.

Approach B:

This is an alternate template. It is similar to the one mentioned above, but with different wording. **What Worked Well (WWW)** and **Even Better If (EBI)**. It is simply a matter of the facilitator's preference.

What Worked Well	Even Better If
Example of a training workshop:	Example of a training workshop:
• *the content of the topic* • *...*	• *there were more visuals in the material* • *...*
Example of a group session:	Example of a group session:
• *the agenda design* • *...*	• *We had more time for exercises in the session* • *...*

Approach C:

This technique is used for gathering information using sticky notes. On a large wall-chart, make either of the templates shown in Approach A or Approach B.

a. Describe the purpose of the AAR session. For the topic of focus, inform the participants that these questions are to be addressed in the format: **I liked** and **I wish** (as an example).

b. Give the participants a stack of large size sticky-notes, and markers to write their responses. Instruct that only one idea be written (legibly!) per sticky note.

c. The individuals then would write their responses and place them on the wall chart at random—in the pre-planned columns such as **I Liked, I Wish,** and **We Learned.**

d. Cluster the sticky note responses into meaningful themes.

I Liked	I Wish	We Learned
Cluster – Theme A*	*Cluster – Theme 1*	*(* Priority) *For each prioritized cluster describe*
Cluster – Theme B	*Cluster -Theme 2**	*lesson learned and ideas for improvement and*
Cluster – Theme C*	*Cluster – Theme 3**	*change*

CONCEPT DIAGRAM

This diagram on the facing page is an example of information gathering using a wall paper or flip chart.

a. Have the participants create sticky notes with one idea per note.

b. Cluster themes with like ideas and label these themes with appropriate titles.

c. Prioritize for improvement. In this case each participant is given three or five paper dots; they vote by placing the dots on items they consider important. I refer to this as a *"Dotocracy"* as in democracy, a way to build consensus on items.

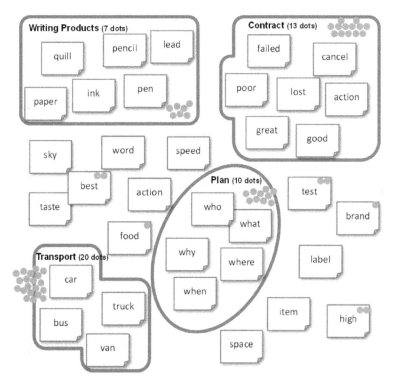

d. Ask volunteers to step up and cluster the sticky-note responses into themes. Have the group discuss the gathered information for a common understanding and then prioritize themes that matter most. For each of these themes, identify lessons learned for future improvement.

e. Assign responsibilities for improvement ideas (or defer for later follow-up).

f. Identify next steps and close the AAR session.

g. After the workshop, document the gathered
    information, summarize the AAR, and
    communicate this to participants and
    stakeholders.

EXAMPLES

EXAMPLE 1

This is an AAR of a one-week personal cruise trip taken
by my wife and me, from New York to Bermuda. The
name of the cruise company is intentionally left out.

I Liked	I Wish
• *The cabin with balcony*	• *Bed had a better mattress*
• *Serving staff was excellent*	• *Food in the buffet was of better quality*
• *The dining room*	• *The ship's interior was dated**
• *Spa service*	
• *The concierge service*	• *The furniture in the state room was more comfortable (especially the chairs)*
• *The port of call – was historic*	• *There were lectures on the sea days*

Summary:

While we enjoyed the cruise, we believe we did not get value for money paid for a better stateroom class. Among the "I Wish" categories, the most important for us next time would be to check on when the ship is refurbished / upgraded. We indicated this by using an asterisk in our list. If it has not been upgraded in the last five years or so, we will not go on it. In addition, we have learned that we can go on the comparison websites and check on the feedback by previous passengers about the quality of the food.

In this real example, which took for my wife and me no more than 15 minutes, we have collectively understood that age of the ship's upgrading is very important to us. Moreover, we have decided to do more research about the cruise line and the venue by going on comparison websites where feedback of previous passengers would be of value.

EXAMPLE 2

This is an example of an AAR of a two-day training in Facilitation Skills that I had conducted. As a trainer and facilitator, I have conducted many such classes. AAR was conducted immediately after the class had concluded. It took about 20 minutes to gather this very important information, which can be used for continuous improvement of the class including the material, venue, and the delivery.

I Liked	I Wish
Effective use of examples and stories – illustrated well	There were more presentations on day-one versus lecture
Recap of tools and techniques every topic	The Categories of topics had detailed descriptions for context setting
Moving the participants around rather than sitting for too long (i.e. physical)	More data is provided in explaining the Facilitation Framework – spend more time
Empowered participants to be in control as guides (i.e. workshop facilitators)	More time was allocated for individual and group exercises
Course content promoted thinking outside-the-box	Feedback was solicited on both days – versus the end of the course
Very little PowerPoint used in training (No "death by PowerPoint")	Make this course pre-requisite for some roles in the organization such as managers
Fast paced; and engaging	Presentations Skills Training could be a pre-requisite for this course
Discussion of remote/virtual facilitation options-even though it is not in scope	The class was held off-site versus the office to avoid distraction
Learning phrases such as "Little learning is big learning" – very effective	The participants workbook was of better quality (the text in some sections was cut off)
Facilitator helped people feel comfortable with activities, engaging business stories, etc.	The workbook was in color instead of black & white print
Group size of 12 is ideal for this class	The workbook was provided in PDF or electronic format as well

At the conclusion of the training class, as an external contractor to the corporation, I had submitted my report to the director of Learning & Development of this organization. I then reviewed this feedback with the corporate training director. We both clustered the information into themes to determine actions for improvement. The themes are noted in the column under I Wish. The theme may be defined as a concept, entity, event, or thing that describes an issue, problem, or an opportunity. Note that in this chart, I use the word "Material" to refer to the content I created for this course.

I Liked	I Wish
Effective use of examples and stories – illustrated well	There were more presentations on day-one versus lecture *(Theme - Material 1)*
Recap of tools and techniques every topic	The Categories of topics had detailed descriptions for context setting *(Theme - Material 2)*
Effective in moving the participants around rather than sitting for too long (i.e. physical)	More data is provided in explaining the Facilitation Framework – spend more time *(Theme - Material 3)*
Empowered participants to be in control as guides (i.e. workshop facilitators)	More time was allocated for individual and group exercises *(Theme - Time)*

I Liked	I Wish
Course content promoted thinking outside-the-box	Feedback was solicited on both days – versus the end of the course *(Theme - Feedback)*
Very little PowerPoint used in training (No "death by PowerPoint")	Make this course a pre-requisite for some roles in the organization such as managers *(Theme - Roles)*
Fast paced; and engaging	Presentations Skills Training could be a pre-requisite for this course *(Theme - Proposal)*
Discussion of remote/virtual facilitation options-even though it is not in scope	The class was held off-site versus the office to avoid distraction *(Theme - Location)*
Learning phrases such as "Little learning is big learning" – very effective	The participants workbook was of better quality (the text in some sections was cut off) *(Theme - Material 4)*
Facilitator helped people feel comfortable with activities, engaging business stories, etc.	The workbook was in color – instead of black & white print *(Theme - Material 5)*
Group size of 12 is ideal for this class	The workbook was provided in PDF or electronic format as well *(Theme - Material 6)*

Actions Taken by the Director:

The items under **I Liked** will be continued by the future class deliveries as before. The items under **I Wish** will be considered for improvement as prioritized below.

Themes	Actions
Material & Time & Feedback	**Material items 1, 2, 3 and 4** will be corrected in the next scheduled class.
	Material 5: The cost of printing colored workbook is high and above the budgeted amount. However, some of the key diagram pages may be printed in color. This will be explored further.
	Material 6: Due to intellectual property (IP) considerations, it is the policy of the organization not to disseminate training material electronically.
	Time: Extra time for exercises will be considered in the course agenda.
	Feedback: Trainers will be asked to include a daily end-of-the-day short AAR exercise so that any needed corrections can be made for the next day class.
Roles	Recommendation will be made to Human Capital Department that all managers should be trained to become facilitators.

Themes	Actions
Proposal	In next year's talent strategy, feasibility will be done to have a presentation skills class as a prerequisite to the facilitation class.
Location	Due to the containment of the cost of the delivery of this class, for now, the classes will continue to be held in the corporate sites.

Communication:

The director then sent the actions and proposals to the appropriate stakeholders for implementation. The director also sent a note of thanks to the students for their AAR input and informed them of the actions being taken.

Conclusion:

Within a few minutes of the conclusion of the class, rich data was gathered as feedback. As a part of continuous improvement, the director in charge acted upon the feedback and communicated to the students as important stakeholders. This builds trust among the providers of feedback that their input was considered valuable for improvements.

This informal *After Action Review* process is a simple but effective continuous improvement tool. The basic skills needed are the understanding of facilitation skills and the rules of brainstorming. While this is an example of a training class, this very technique can be used in any program of knowledge transfer, seminars, focus groups, etc.

EXAMPLE 3

This is an example of an AAR of a two-day workshop that focused on improving a critical process for manufacturing medical devices. There were 15 participants from many different departments. The group was professionally facilitated.

I Liked	I Wish
Interaction among the particulates from various functional areas	There was more time – an additional day to work on the details *
Collaboration for solutions and strategies	There were other important stakeholders from all functional areas *
Open and honest discussion	Do this process with another department
That everyone participated fully	There was room suited for visual displays *
That everyone was willing to resolve issues	
The sustainable action plan	
Facilitated workshop with workable agenda	

The facilitator and the workshop manager had asked for a priority ranking what would matter most in the "I wish" column. The participants identified three items for improvement in the future (shown with asterisks). The result of the AAR was reviewed by the sponsor. It was agreed that any future business workshops would be more effective by ensuring these areas were addressed in the following manner:

- Instead of two-day workshop, time should be allocated for three days so that the participants don't have to rush (and cut short the third day to catch out of town flights).

- Identify all functional areas that touch the process or business area of focus and invite their relevant stakeholders at the appropriate level of responsibility.

- There were many paper charts to be put on the walls as output of the work. The hotel did not have enough wall space and besides they did not like the idea of putting charts on the walls—even with safe masking tape. It was agreed to search for a better conference facilitation-friendly room for the next workshop.

The After Action Review exercise tool less than 30 minutes to complete and yet yielded valuable improvement ideas for future workshops, which would be more effective for the organization, and better value for resources utilized.

OTHER POSSIBILITIES

The informal After Action Review is a very simple tool to use. Its use is limited by our imagination only. From personal use to non-profit organizations, for-profit entities or governmental agencies, this technique can provide improvement opportunities in just about every activity. Some examples for use of AAR include:

- Meetings

- Workshops

- Fund raising events

- Community programs

- Social events

- Technical solutions

- Business solutions

- Governmental initiatives

- Any human endeavor of value

AFTER ACTION REVIEW REPORT TEMPLATE

The benefit of AAR is realized when the output of the workshop is shared with other teams and projects. A summary should be compiled by the manager in charge of AAR and communicated to the project team and other stakeholders who can benefit from it. Timeliness of this communication is important because the participants want to see that the effort put into the AAR has been valued and benefits the organization overall as early as possible.

A template such as the one below can be used for both formal and informal AAR.

AAR Report

Project/Activity/Event Name:

Date & Location of AAR:

Purpose and Scope:

Provide an overview of the activity as a context and the scope of what was included.

Participants:

Include their names and titles, along with their roles in the AAR.

What worked well and why?

Include ideas for ensuring success in the future

What can be improved and how?

Include what can be improved and recommendation for actions.

CHAPTER 4
Formal After Action Review

Typically, the formal After Action Review method is used for activities with larger scope. This can include construction projects, product launches, new legislation rollouts, or new public or private industry programs.

In Information Technology, the after action review process is sometimes called the Post Implementation Review. Likewise, depending upon the nature of the industry or profession, the concept of After Action Review may be referred to by a different name. Sometimes, the term "conducting a Post Mortem" is used. This implies that the activity-in-focus will be "dissected" to understand what happened and what can be learned from it.

In this guide, I provide a generic method that can be customized to suit a specific need. Unlike the Informal AAR where some light knowledge and experience of facilitation and brainstorming could suffice, in the formal AAR, an experienced facilitator is needed to help design the workshop scope, agenda, and approach and then conduct the session.

In some organizations, the line managers must be trained in facilitation; in others, it is best to engage an external facilitator. It can be a matter of organizational culture and practice.

APPROACH

WORKSHOP SESSION PLAN

The project manager/team leader in collaboration with the sponsor of the Activity-in-Focus is in charge of the AAR process.

a. *Establish the AAR objective.* Identify the description and scope of activity for which an AAR is to be conducted. The activity can be a factory has been built, a new product has been launched, governmental legislation has been instituted, a computer system has been rolled out, or a disaster such as a hurricane has to be assessed for post-event situation.

b. *Identify and engage a facilitator (internal or external).* A qualified and experienced neutral facilitator should be preferred. The facilitator does not have to be a subject matter expert, but needs to know enough about the business area of the Activity-in-Focus from the facilitation point of view.

c. *Review the plan of the Activity-in-Focus.* Determine what was planned and what actually occurred.

d. *Identify the participants.* All stakeholders who had direct involvement and responsibility of parts of the Activity-in-Focus.

e. *Identify material to be used in the AAR workshop.* This would include various stakeholders to be assigned to make presentations of the relevant aspects to be addressed in the AAR workshop. For example, in the construction of a manufacturing facility, the areas to be addressed can include site selection, engineering, contracts, construction, equipment installation, and hiring and training of employees.

f. *Select a facilitation-friendly facility.* A qualified facilitator would make a judgment of workshop timeframe and location. These estimates are based on number of participants and an initial approach to facilitating the session.

g. *Establish venue and publish agenda.* The project manager assisted by the facilitator would create and communicate the agenda for the participants. Venue logistics and resource needs would be initiated.

FACILITATION AGENDA

Based on the agreed agenda, and in collaboration with the sponsor, manager, and/or key stakeholders, the facilitator would prepare a detailed agenda known as a *Running Order Agenda (ROA)*, also called an *Annotated Agenda*. This is only shared with the project manager and not with the participants. The ROA is a systematic description of how the workshop would be conducted. It describes how to prepare presentation materials and determine requirements for facilitation supplies.

AAR WORKSHOP

- Review the objectives of the AAR with the participants

- Review the Activity-in-Focus, its status, and relevant details for common understanding

- Facilitate session and capture relevant information in an organized manner

- Agree on the documentation, communication, and dissemination plan of the workshop output

- Close the AAR session

Following is a Methodology Template for planning and conducting a formal AAR.

TEMPLATES

PLANNING TEMPLATE

The Methodology Template may be used as a guide by the individual in charge of the Activity-in-Focus to plan the AAR.

#	Approach	What	How
1	Pre-Workshop Preparation	Gain commitment to conduct an AAR from the sponsor of the Activity-in-Focus (AIF) initiative and or key stakeholders.	Make a proposal for the AIF (it may be a project, an initiative, or an event). Also consider identifying "Themes" or Clusters of main topics relevant to the AIF.
2	What were we trying to do?	Describe the objective and expected outcomes of the AIF.	Prepare a presentation on behalf of management and the key stakeholders – giving facts.
3	What actually happened?	Describe the result of the AIF contribution.	Presentation of facts by all directly involved in the AIF. The facts may be clustered into themes.

#	Approach	What	How
4	What did I like?	Individual contribution to the topic—both facts and opinion: "I Liked…" or "What Worked Well" ideas.	Gather information from individual participants around the themes.
5	What would I do differently?	Individual contribution to the topic both facts and opinion: "I Wish…" or "Even Better If" ideas.	Gather information from individual participants around the themes.
6	What lessons have we learned and what do we recommend to be done differently?	Groups take each of the themes and identify lessons learned and make recommendations for each lesson (all participants).	Groups provide specific and tangible recommendations for action. Tools: Provide a *"Lessons and Recommendation"* common template
7	How would we evaluate the lessons and their recommendations?	Group Brainstorm	Define guiding principles for the recommendations
8	Prioritize Recommendations	Develop criteria for prioritization in a group brainstorm.	Recommendations to be documented on themes and priorities.

#	Approach	What	How
9	Recommendation Actions	Draft specific initiatives to be taken. Determine documentation, storage, and dissemination of AAR outputs for sharing knowledge.	Identify Key Stakeholders, Business Area Ownership, and Dependencies.
10	Key Stakeholder Communication	Develop summary message and recommendations; Develop communication plan.	Next step action. Tools: Develop a Summary Template for communication.
11	Wrap-up and Close Session		

FACILITATOR'S RUNNING ORDER AGENDA TEMPLATE

This Methodology Template may be used as a guide for the initial design of his/her Activity-in-Focus AAR facilitation.

Review Activity-in-Focus AIF objective, outcomes and themes of the topics based on the type of the subject matter and industry (the workshop constitutes all participants invited to the AAR)	Theme Owners / Leads to provide overview of their themes for a common understanding (*Theme*: May be defined as a concept, entity, event, or a thing – which describes an issue, problem, or an opportunity)

Have the group discuss each theme and identify if any additional themes are needed	Write on large sticky notes and place on the wall chart or a flip chart.
Prioritize themes for detailed analysis	The group prioritizes the themes from most impactful to least. Identify the top 3 to 5 or more themes for detailed analysis ("what worked well and what could be done better").
Conduct Root Cause Analysis for each theme	Use Fishbone/Ishikawa technique (See Chapter 1). Use flipchart for each template. Brainstorm in sub-teams and identify candidates for recommendations. For any cross-functional item, write it on a sticky note and hand it over to the appropriate theme owner for them to include in their effort.
Document detailed recommendations for each theme	The recommendation should be Actionable, Specific, and Clear. (Provide any supporting references e.g., relevant industry practices documents). Create Terms Glossary for any unique terms or acronyms being used.
Each theme-sub-group reports out	Each group reports out on their root causes/recommendations (takes questions & discussions from the group).

Group agreement on next steps	The larger group further prioritizes among the themes and recommendations. Assign roles for documenting the agreed outcomes. Agree on next steps for communicating the AAR result for the benefit of others.
Venue and supplies	Ensure a facilitation-friendly room, secure necessary facilitation supplies for all aspects of the workshop activities, and develop a detailed step-by-step Running Order Agenda. Facilitate the workshop.

SUMMARY BY THEMES TEMPLATE

Team:

Team Owner:
Date:

Purpose: *Describe the context and scope of this theme. What we have learned and what we will do with the lessons learned.*

Instructions for Sub-Team Leads:

1) Review your area of AAR information and analysis
2) Being the subject matter expert, evaluate key points and identify the major themes
3) For each theme, determine actionable recommendation(s) which can be used by other such initiatives.

Example - The feedback from "Training" Theme: (The example of an AAR conducting upon completion of a new factory).

- *The training provided to the*
- *Recommendation: As there are three shifts, it would be practical*

		Major Theme	Recommendation
	new employees was not timely and therefore there was down-time and loss of productivity	*to provide train-the-trainer orientation to the shift managers giving them freedom to provide training to the workers proactively*	
1	Training Shift Workers		
2	Reward & Recognition for Excellence		
3			
4			
5			

EXAMPLE

An international food manufacturing organization had built a multi-million-dollar, state-of-the-art factory. Their management planned and conducted a three-day After Action Review workshop to capture lessons or conclusions that could benefit other factories in different parts of the world. The management of this newly built factory had outlined their mission as follows:

Objective:

- Capture and share lessons or conclusions of the new plant initiative

- Validate what we have learned, and offer best practice design considerations for manufacturing sites elsewhere

Goal:

Drive value. Produce actionable output (i.e. lessons, conclusions, and recommendations), including what we should do differently

Steps:

- Initiate After Action Review

- Develop AAR Pre-Work Information Gathering

- Establish Works Team by "Theme" category. (Themes were identified for workstream groups: Engineering, Land & Site, R & D, Security, Quality, Buying Service, Finance, Business Systems, and Hiring & Training.)

- Gather Information on Conclusions and Summary Themes for Recommendations

- Plan, Design and Conduct a two-day Face-to-Face Workshop: a) Conduct AAR Workshop and Document Outputs b) Plan Post-Workshop Activity: Compilation, Storage, and Dissemination of output for Knowledge Sharing

Execution:

Using the Methodology Template, a detailed plan was developed by the management sponsor executive, project manager and a professional facilitator. The facilitator then designed a detailed agenda using the Methodology Template Running Order Agenda. Pre-Work was given to the work teams to develop after action details *(I liked, I wish, We learned)*.

The recommendations were made by each work team using the Summary by Themes Template. Next the project manager and sponsor summarized the result of the AAR for their senior management to share the lessons and conclusions across the organization to benefit other planned factories.

OTHER POSSIBILITIES

Per the criteria outlined in Chapter 2, there are unlimited possibilities for conducting a Formal AAR. Here are just a few examples:

- Rollout of a new product or service

- Implementation of a governmental legislation

- Building of a school building

- Implementation of a new computer system

- Enhancement of facilities for a community

Resources

Books by the Author Artie Mahal

1) *Facilitator's and Trainer's Toolkit, Engage and Energize Participants in Meetings, Classes and Workshops*

2) *How Work Gets Done, Business Process Management Basics and Beyond,*

Facilitation Supply Sources

BusinessBalls	www.businessballs.com (Tools and Templates) UK.
Grove	http://www.grove.com/site/index.html. (Graphics Supplies, USA)
HRD Central	http://www.hrdcentral.com/ (Australia)
Neuland	www.neuland.com (Australia, Europe, North America)
Office Oxygen	www.officeoxygen.com (Workplace tools, North America)
Pinipoint-Facilitation	www.pinpoint-facilitatioon.com (UK partners with Neuland)
The Training Shop	www.thetrainingshop.co.uk (UK)
Trainers Warehouse	www.trainerswarehouse.com (North America)

Professional Forums

International Association of Facilitators (IAF) www.iaf-world.org

International Association of Facilitators (IAF Europe) www.iaf-europe-mena.org

www.ingramcontent.com/pod-product-compliance
Lightning Source LLC
Chambersburg PA
CBHW071552080326
40690CB00056B/1802